CHAIRS IN THE RIVER

Laura Bayless

FUTURECYCLE PRESS
www.futurecycle.org

Copyright © 2017 Laura Bayless
All Rights Reserved

Published by FutureCycle Press
Athens, Georgia, USA

ISBN 978-1-942371-39-7

Don't let the past steal your present.
—Cherralea Morgen

In gratitude for my poetry sisters,
Jennifer and Kate

Contents

Memorial Beach	7
The Company of Birds	8
Time Out	9
Submerged	10
Chairs in the River	11
Ragamuffin	12
Sometimes a Word	13
Invent Your World	14
Redemption	15
Sure Cure	16
Confectionery	17
Still	18
Recognition	19
Diamonds or Stones	20
Two of a Kind	21
What Happens	22
Poetic Terminators	23
Faith	24
Left Behind	25
Aberrant Poet	26
Prophetic	27
Luminary	28
Unrevealed	29
The Poem That Rises from Sleep	30
Moonlighting	31
Ghostly Winter	32
January Morning	33
August	34
Passages	35
Whose Hands	36
Numbers	37
Forethought of Grief	38
Soon Enough	39
Solitary Serenity	40
When I'm Ready to Go	41
Humbled	42

Memorial Beach

All that is past possesses our present.
—John Fowles

This morning, on a long strand
of empty seashore, only my footprints
mar the powdery brown sediment,
coarse canvas for my shadow.
A slim form under the surface
resembles a shallow grave.

Vast blue, calm today, frames
scarred and rutted logs, artful
strands of tangled kelp, seaweed nests,
water-weathered cypress limbs.
Two egrets wander at river's end,
solace for my siblings long gone.
Solitary gray and white gull
perches nearby on one foot.

Single empty mussel shell lies
in the lifeline crack of a stone palm.
Hollow-pitted boulders bracket
braided ropes of coffee-colored flotsam.
Stirred by elemental debris,
everything recollected opens me.
Out at sea whales gush wellsprings,
pass south on instinctive journeys.
I turn my back to the sea,
consider what might be possible
on this first day of a new year.

The Company of Birds

White-crowned sparrows
and one plump California towhee
come to the glass door,
beg like tramps
on a cold April morning.

A wrentit and hooded junco
moonwalk and bop
near the feeder,
dip their small beaks,
scatter seeds across the deck.

These past few days,
predictably gray
with a chill wind,
do nothing to confiscate
the anniversaries of my heart.

Memory loaded
with unforgotten faces,
empty chairs,
I pull my blanket closer,
tuck myself into false warmth,
wait for sleep to overtake
relics of loss.

Time Out

At the summit of Whaler's Knoll
I survey a portion of coastline,
single egret, sleeping harbor seal,
line of pelicans skimming across
the sea in fluid formation.

I feel the sun on my arm,
an ache in my lower back,
rumble of hunger
before I dig into my lunch
of apple and cheese,
ripe cherries, almonds.

I need more time
to watch breakers roll in,
crest beyond islands of stone,
bear the tremor in my bones,
listen to white foam sigh.

I'm in no hurry
to budge from my hilltop refuge,
trek back down through the woods
to the rugged north shore,
return to whatever consequence
I've left behind.

Submerged

Motionless great blue heron,
afloat on driftwood, meditates.

Silver-furred seal sleeps
atop a stone shelf in Whaler's Cove.

Wild iris sway on slender stems,
yield purple pinwheels.

Dark doorway, entrance to inner earth,
appears beneath a jagged crag.

Gaping sandstone mouths hum
weathered songs from seaside cliffs.

Blue ceanothus, early blossoms
garland thickets in late February.

Wind stirs tears, salty echoes
of unhealed sorrows.

Breadth of horizon condenses
my world to this moment.

Chairs in the River

Three weathered wooden chairs
sit empty facing each other,
a conversation arrangement
recalling sounds of laughter
and banter one might hear,
muted now into the whirr of water
flowing over a bank of stones.

Sunlight through cottonwoods
pools shadows across the seats.
Wet stains creep up the legs,
like cityscapes at dawn,
the outline of tall buildings.
A cluster of large and small rocks
lies half-submerged in the stream.
Ripples, fluid messages, slide
under silent chairs.

Nearby a branch with teardrop leaves
hovers a few feet above
the westward-drifting river.
On the other bank a fallen sycamore trunk
collects debris from winter storms,
rests like a broken arm against a redwood.

Though you might claim this place
your green temple where sequins gleam
on vibrations of the brook in motion,
this is my Big Sur landmark
where childhood memories surface
and wash downstream.

Ragamuffin

Towhead in scruffy cutoffs,
worn sneakers, smudged nose,
remains of a Sugar Daddy sucker
stuck to a corner of her mouth,
she collects shells from Otter Cove,
lays them inside a beach towel
in the silver basket of her
twice-hand-me-down Schwinn.

She's gone to the shore again,
slipped out the garage door
when Mother wasn't looking,
raced to the corner,
spun in the gravel before pedaling off
down Beach Street to Ocean View
to count hermit crabs, starfish
that inhabit her coastal castles,
granite fortresses where
she can be something
other than a good girl.

Sometimes a Word

Emily D says *sometimes*
I write a word and look at it
until it begins to shine.

I write *barefoot* on my page.
watch it take form,
sole, skin, and toes
that have never grown older,
no more than seven or eight,
with grass stains, sand
between the littlest toe
and its neighbor.

Sunburn across the top
reveals a red map that fades
as days drift toward September.
Along the arch impressions
of pebbles remain and on the heel
the white gauze of a blister.

My word has lasted all day
without stocking or shoe,
still wants to dance
across a cool green lawn
until sunlight finds
its way into dusk.

Invent Your World

Because you might deem
it would be ungrateful
to waste a whole day
without at least
one original thought...

you go outside
before the sun slips
over the hilltop
east of the valley,
breathe in dusty scent
of autumn, gather
an acorn or two
to place beside
the curled sycamore
leaf you will save
from your next walk
in the meadow.

You are imagining
a shrine to a season
of gilded serenity
and unraveling time.

Redemption

At the raw edge of the hillside
where wind scours
flakes of shale to whiteness,
nothing grows.

Onto the slope
below the bare rim,
I toss
each remnant of foliage,
bud and leaf, seed
stem
blossoms
when they fade.

From this compost
what has perished
may or may not resurrect.

Sure Cure

Feeling bluesy on a Saturday morning,
so far down in the dumps
I'm reduced to watching Tom & Jerry
cartoons on Nickelodeon,
I decide to take a cruise down the coast
in my Mustang convertible, top down,
wind in my hair, 1200 on the AM dial,
KYAA cranked up on the stereo,
DJ Chuck "Boom Boom" Cannon blasting
the Oldies with *Roll Over Beethoven*.

Tires hugging Highway One curves
I wave at strangers in yellow Lamborghinis,
pass tourists fighting
the wind at Hurricane Point,
grumble about behemoth rental RVs,
sing along with *Rockin' Pneumonia
and the Boogie Woogie Flu* by Johnny Rivers.

Ten bucks worth of gas and 24 miles later
I make a U-turn, brooding like Rumi
hoping for some spiritual insight,
head back to Carmel for frozen yogurt
with Karen Carpenter's
I'm On the Top of the World
on the radio as the only remaining blues
stretch out west across the sea.

Confectionery

In *Sweet Offerings* my feet
refuse to stand still
as I hear an old jukebox song
coming from behind
the glass-front candy counters,
Buddy Holly singing
That'll Be the Day.
Another shop entertains
with piped-in rhythm and blues.
I realize I cannot NOT dance,
cannot deny the drum beat,
the frivolous familiar tunes.

I dance in the oddest places,
feel only slightly embarrassed
      or not at all,
having somehow outgrown caring
what strangers might consider
as peculiar or improper.
I will never be invited
to dance the jive with the stars,
don't require a live band,
take rhythm where I find it,
rock and roll through life.

Still

If you sit very still on a sandbank
along the Carmel River,
you begin to separate
scraps of sounds around you.

You hear that chattering jay
you cannot see, a seven-note songbird,
a particular *chir-chirp,* whistling
you wish you could identify.

Nearby horsetail ferns whisper.
Riversound ripples
over rocky streambed shallows.
Wind in the treetops purrs.
Crossed branches creak,
rub against one another.

If you stay long enough,
you might see a mother goose
lead five downy yellow goslings
upriver, father trailing behind.

You could delay leaving
on the off chance more magic's
about to happen—
finally notice cottonwoods
shedding summer snowflakes.

Recognition

>After the poem *Lonely* by Amy Brewster

You reach for the opaque blue,
how it arrives a half-hour
before dawn, before your body
braces to accept one more day.

You wait for a sign, the edge
of tomorrow just a vague thought.
You observe the gilded rim
of brown hills in the east,
rise and boil water for tea,
place a spoon in your mug
so it will not crack,
so cold overnight.

How many hands perform
this same task, grasp
the warm side of a cup,
begin another day alone
beneath an empty sky?

Diamonds or Stones

Just nineteen, I agreed to marry,
chose a diamond ring
at Sears Roebuck with
matching set of gold circlets.
Eleven years later divorce
followed his shocking infidelity.

After ten years single,
I venture to wed again.
The second diamond
ring combined engagement
and wedding, singular band
meant to represent unity.

When the stone came loose,
slipped down the shower drain,
practicality demanded I exhume
my first solitaire so nearly
the same size and perfection.
A jeweler skillfully reset it.
I wore that ring for seventeen years
until my second trip to court
to dispense with another fickle man.

I keep the reminder in a crystal bowl,
take it out occasionally to see
if it still fits, if I still care or not.
Perhaps I should have realized
you ought not to replace
one faithless husband with another.

Two of a Kind

Two ivory-colored doves land
on my deck, implore my generosity,
extra portion of birdseed.
They have lost their natural shyness,
seem to trust I am altruistic.

This brace of mourning doves,
with thin black neck rings
like matrimonial promises,
cautiously approach each day,
easily startled into abrupt flight
by the sudden arrival of a scrub jay
with menacing white eyebrows.

There's something tender
about their visits, a pair
more brave together.
They step carefully along the rail,
arrive at my weathered wicker table,
nip delicately at seeds lodged
between fissures in old wood slats.

I have a fondness for the couple,
for their fidelity, shared understanding
of life's invitations and dangers.
As one living alone I take
solace from such mated visitations.

What Happens

to the ones who fall out of favor,
who go on alone while
their spouses move on
with new lovers, fresh partners?

How do you learn to arrive single
somewhere meant for pairs,
where the price of admission
is $25 for one, $40 per couple?
Somehow not being two of a kind
involves an unjust expense,
another unintended consequence
of having been abandoned.

You become the fifth wheel
at a table for four.
Perhaps it gets easier after
you overhear a woman gripe
about her husband's amnesia
regarding closing cupboard doors,
or maybe the man grumbles about
his wife's obsession with jewelry.
You realize they fight constantly.

You begin to value the freedom
to follow your own desires
without answering to a mate,
grow fond of your own company,
recall there's one thing
worse than being alone…

wishing you were.

Poetic Terminators

You write in solitude, long hours,
often doubt your natural gift,
tenaciously retract and revise,
consider a poem complete,
desire an impartial opinion.

A friend invites you to a critique
with local poets, sounds promising.
You're blindsided from the start.
One man begins with a negative comment,
questions your topic, every other word.
He doesn't understand your premise.

You sign up for a seminar,
perhaps a workshop
where feedback is offered.
You bring your best work.
It's your turn in hot water.

The published MFA poet
advertised in the flyer
begins by declaring your tree
can't be joyful; inanimate
objects don't have emotions.
He wants to change the voice
from you to I, waxes professorial.
You're disillusioned, in shock.

There's a woman who never reads
other poets, suggests change of setting,
time frame, wants to eliminate any
big words she has to look up in a dictionary.
Another nitpicks all your adjectives.

You find them everywhere, the fussbudgets,
at festivals, writing groups, conferences.
They offer a whole raft of useless suggestions,
demolish your hard-earned lyricism.

Still, you write!

Faith

> *That which we cannot name is lost to us.*
> —Greg Levoy

I lose faith in words,
no language supple enough
to describe an arching branch,
no speech for the ephemeral
flourish of a budding stem.

My words murmur
mistaken thoughts,
cannot resolve what
does not belong,
have gone in search
of a clearing ground,
a way to say how evening
stumbles under folding sky.

I mistrust the promise
of introspective expressions
or a profound declaration
for endless grief.
Still I tinker with syllable
and riddle, blunder endlessly,
hope to originate
a more precise truth.

Left Behind

I regret what doesn't get written,
words that arrive while walking
yet vanish by the time
I return to pen and paper.

I forfeit landscape narratives,
a dragonfly as it washes
its slender front legs,
journey of a caterpillar with black face
and twenty miniscule legs,
glitter in sand and stone,
images that sigh and murmur
with symbolic metaphors.

Fat bumblebees drone above
patterns of tumbled leaves,
cause me to slow down,
mindful of what's left behind,
suggestions of significance.

What doesn't get written
is harder to catch than sunbeams.
I toss phrases out to the tempo
of my steps, hope rhythm
will bind them to my mind.

Aberrant Poet

She's elusive, in constant transformation
without form or answers.
She doesn't ask *why,* knows reasons change.

You'll find her in a breeze,
behind globe lilies in a fern-thick glade,
coming up from night into daybreak,
following the sun down to sea.

She feels like the dust
of fall leaves crushed in your hand,
like the first sip of cold water
along the length of your throat.

Born in a cradle of unspoken sorrows
half past her life, she reads
deep waters, hillside foliage,
surveys spaces between periwinkle petals.

She lives in undersea canyons,
on mountaintops, in shoreline mists,
travels on a single hawk feather
or silk of a flying spider at dawn.

She exists to write down something
you didn't know you wanted to know
until you traced her lines
with the brush of your heart.

Prophetic

The muse comes dressed
in verdigris and gray,
mystic soothsayer
of present and future.

A small grove of cypress
on a knoll overlooking the ocean
unfurls hoary witch's hair.
Gnarled, interlaced limbs embrace
like women rooted
in their coastal birthplace,
holding the family together.

Broad branches persist.
Long weather-worn arms
brush early spring grass,
a suggestion of lifetimes
apparent in yet-strong frame.
Some of their fallen lie nearby,
a shipwreck tangle of trunks,
sculptured silver bones.

I compare the ashen hue
of my hair to tattered lace lichen,
muscles in my lower back
to grain and seam in the trees,
all holding the body together
in the face of age.

Luminary

Breakers bellow on Moonstone Beach,
drown out other sounds.
The dark rocky sand offers
rough multicolored jewels
for my pockets.

Light near water
paints the air,
dances silver stars
on the surface of the sea,
a scintillation reflected
on tiny polished pebbles
that shift beneath my feet.

I become light's priestess
and she my muse.
Foam leaves behind swaths
of diamond chips,
erased again and again—
the endless consoling ritual
of shimmering salt tears

that do not last for long.

Unrevealed

Before dawn mourning doves call
to one another, a lonely sort
of overtone, two or three syllable
responses in lingering silver mist.

Their melodic consultation occurs
among shadows, within oak limbs
and gray-blue eucalyptus leaves,
the seclusion of early morning.

First light paints subtle tracings
across north-facing mountains.
Dove harmonies and my thoughts
reside in between at this hour,
as if we are the unseen phases
on the other side of the moon,
imperceptible except to ourselves.

The Poem That Rises from Sleep

I am the poem that rises from sleep
to pace the hallway
because my thoughts
are crowded with doubt.

I am the poem that rises from sleep
to walk outside, stand
in shadowed hours past midnight,
black sea above
alive with faraway eyes.

I am the poem that rises from sleep
to search for the perfect thumbnail
of moon that lingers over mountains
in the west toward morning.

I am the poem that returns to dreams
trailing moonbeams
from the soles of my feet
to tuck among the quilts.

I am the poem that wakes
to the risk of another day,
not knowing if night's travels
are enough to salt the coming hours
with leftover sparks of stars.

Moonlighting

As if by some inner clock
I wake at 4:15,
pull on robe and slippers,
grab a quilt, go out
to sit in my deck chair,
watch the April eclipse.

The moon, half-covered
in mid-month phase, spills
beams along the west edge,
a bright candle flame
in my night sky.

The flare fades away.
Starlight multiplies, pinpoints gleam
within an indigo stratum.
The dark circle of full moon
remains even as the residual border
of moonlight shrinks, dissolves.

This is the lunar enchantment
of astronomical alterations
occurring as seasons evolve,
spring and fall magicians
of the cosmos, a bewitching
sphere above planet earth.

Ghostly Winter

*I try to apply colors like words that shape poems,
like notes that shape music.*
—Joan Miro

Colorless forms gather,
a collection of watery altostratus
with imprecise edges, all illusion,
contours and coves circumscribed
only briefly west to east.

On an early December day,
palest gray flannel on chalk-white
montage of winter clouds
offers blurred interpretation
but no authentic storm.

Pine, oak, even rosemary
that tumbles down the hillside,
slowly leach of summer-day color.
If you were to take on the mood
of such lackluster weather,
you might curl up on the davenport
with your favorite fleece blanket,
forgo venturing out into
an indeterminate world...

but, no, the day beckons.

January Morning

I open my eyes today,
hold a grateful thought
that obscures any contradictions
regarding time and climate,
solitary dilemmas.

Weather analysts predict
the overcast will leave
by noon, sunshine to follow,
continuing drought, about which
I can do nothing, except

celebrate greenness
where the deer tribe has grazed
since the December rain,
listen to black chatter
of crows in the eucalyptus.

Unblemished by seasonal fires,
mountains to the south
and east abide, fertile for now.

What more would I ask for
except to banish dark notions,
the self-destructive debate
about irreversible
wounds of infidelity and loss?

August

One afternoon in August
a friend and I stand
under a blooming magnolia,
inhale the thick perfume,
watch bees gather pollen
from centers of unfolding petals.

In a patch of berry vines
rows of leafy hedges conceal
gems of yellow raspberries.
I reach in and pluck
one pale honey-colored jewel
that pulls free from its core,
place it in my mouth.
Still warm late in the day
its sweetness dissolves
the length of my tongue.

Down along a green corridor
in pursuit of more
I gather one after another
nectared gold treat,
roll them from cheek to cheek,
let them melt
like sugar bubbles
in the sun of my mouth.

Passages

Wispy white veils drift
across blue linen sky
over a parched meadow.

We are between hours,
an afternoon's interlude
on a November day.

Quietness overcomes rustling weeds,
whatever worrisome thoughts
remain from morning.

Early rain has edged
the pasture with tufted green,
a stitching of fallen leaves.

Sunlight casts lustrous ribbons
through sapling branches,
gilds our passage.

Companions of nature,
we feel no different
than arroyo willows.

Whose Hands

I can't remember the exact day
when my hands altered
at wrinkles along my wrist,
became the hands I watched
my mother lay upon the arm
of her favorite recliner.
I took note of channeled veins,
brown age spots, a scar or two,
same rucked knuckles,
the damage and fragility
her years had worn into
a mosaic composition.

I don't know why
on that particular day
it became clear we were
women on the same journey.
I discovered my place
somewhere within an equivalent life.
How many of the same tasks,
kindred forms of affection,
comparable moments of grief
were frayed into our timelines,
traced on two poignant thumbs.

Numbers

I've lived long enough
to count my dead on both hands
a woman says, and I start to count,
already knowing two hands
are not enough to calculate
a multilayered sweep of grief.

I add up the colors
of their eyes, simple things
like how they tied their shoes
or carried their shadows,
hours and days gone.

It's a strange thing—
these sorrows that never
go away, never completely
sidetrack to some
comfortable stillness.

I imagine a hollow heart
where there's no echo
from conversations
I have with myself
when I'm alone
or on the anniversary
of a departure,
a mute language of numbers.

Forethought of Grief

One day in October
I decide to visit the four
side by side graves
on a green knoll
overlooking Monterey Bay.
I don't come often,
don't really think of them
as *there* among the rows
of bronze plaques,
vases of plastic flowers.
They were laid to rest
one by one, none recent,
the first over fifty years ago.

Nostalgia always the same,
his cigarette burning down
in the glass ashtray
on the stand by his red chair,
afternoons at the hairdresser
to arrange her silver-white curls,
his series of classic Matchbox cars,
her chubby hand
banging on her highchair.

For a time I stand in silence,
wait to hear the breathy hush
of waves along the bay shore.
Still my old bitterness returns,
the deep throb of revisiting
so much loss in one place.

Soon Enough

Oh death is waiting for me...
—Federico Garcia Lorca

Sometimes without warning
grief revisits, awakens old sorrows,
brings back intimate images
of my sweet toddler son
still in blue flannel pajamas
and his beloved little sister,
who followed him in death
the very next year.

Even though their photographs
on the bookshelf are badly faded,
I picture them as they were,
boy counting his toy cars,
small girl in pink overalls
exploring a mud puddle
or tossing her spoon to the floor,
imagine them watched over
by my parents and sisters.

Long ago my lost ones came
in dreams, offered reassurance,
but muted recall is what remains.
Death is waiting for me,
a tender reunion I desire.
I trust my leaving finally
becomes the way to reconcile.

Solitary Serenity

Pencil in hand, notebook beneath
the bridge of my wrist,
mumble and flourish of small waves
scrolling ashore, quiet
afternoon contentment.

Better this solitary serenity
than an uneasy alliance
just to fill the hours.
I rest against a bleached log,
examine its dark-knotted eye
that stares from a white skull.
Sun, warm on my face,
drives the gray wall of mist
further out to sea.

A continual glittering chain
of cars pulses the artery of Highway 1
just beyond my peripheral vision.
Sunlight's radiant path shimmers
across ocean's constant motion.
Miniature craters dimple the sand
with late afternoon shadows.

Day prepares to surrender
in a way mortal creatures never do.
I come back to the coastal shoreline
in search of neutrality,
less questions,
more enduring beauty.
The Pacific never disappoints.

When I'm Ready to Go

take me to the greensward, the woodland dale
beyond the tangle of supple willow spurs

where a footbridge crosses the river
that mirrors a few bleached-yarn clouds.

Tag along to where tiny purple-white
pagodas crop up among late spring grasses.

Let me get deliriously lost in a secret ravine
where fiesta flowers cling to my legs

so I can gather wood mint for tea,
let the hairy fringe pod keep its secrets.

I want to tread trails deer forge through
underbrush that crowds the oak forest

and talk with the fractured scarecrow
husk of an old pine stump.

Allow me time to linger beside owl's clover
and lime-green tresses of maidenhair fern,

admire saffron sun-kissed lichen on a fallen log,
follow a wandering cabbage white butterfly.

Then leave me where the buckeye torches
circulate their vanilla scent in May and

cast off chestnut-colored spheres in fall
onto the backyard fringe of a sunlit meadow.

Humbled

> *Blessed are they who see beautiful things
> in humble places.*
> —Camille Pissarro

Dazzling skies after long
hours of overnight rain
intensify my winter ramble.

Box elder leaf shadows flutter
along a meandering path,
resemble blue butterflies.

Sequins sparkle on oaks.
Two creamy doves nibble
wild lilac blossoms.

Dewdrops in sunbeams
on long-bladed grass
flaunt rainbow prisms.

Moss-cloaked boulder shelters
three death-angel mushrooms.
Sycamore and eucalyptus leaves
fashion paisley designs on forest floor.

I bless the ache along my left hip
that lets me know I am alive.

Acknowledgments

These poems, some in other versions, first appeared in the following publications.

Avocet: "Passages" (titled "Crossings")
Blue Heron Review: "Luminary"
Homestead Review: "Time Out," "Chairs in the River," "Sure Cure," "Solitary Serenity," "The Poem That Rises from Sleep"
Nomad's Choir: "Unrevealed"
Porter Gulch Review: "August"
Song of the San Joaquin: "Redemption"

Cover artwork, artistic treatment by Diane Kistner of a photo by Jenny Wolf; author photo by Jeff Clothier; cover and interior book design by Diane Kistner; Georgia text and titling

About FutureCycle Press

FutureCycle Press is dedicated to publishing lasting English-language poetry books, chapbooks, and anthologies in both print-on-demand and Kindle ebook formats. Founded in 2007 by long-time independent editor/publishers and partners Diane Kistner and Robert S. King, the press incorporated as a nonprofit in 2012. A number of our editors are distinguished poets and writers in their own right, and we have been actively involved in the small press movement going back to the early seventies.

The FutureCycle Poetry Book Prize and honorarium is awarded annually for the best full-length volume of poetry we publish in a calendar year. Introduced in 2013, our Good Works projects are anthologies devoted to issues of universal significance, with all proceeds donated to a related worthy cause. Our Selected Poems series highlights contemporary poets with a substantial body of work to their credit; with this series we strive to resurrect work that has had limited distribution and is now out of print.

We are dedicated to giving all of the authors we publish the care their work deserves, making our catalog of titles the most diverse and distinguished it can be, and paying forward any earnings to fund more great books.

We've learned a few things about independent publishing over the years. We've also evolved a unique, resilient publishing model that allows us to focus mainly on vetting and preserving for posterity poetry collections of exceptional quality without becoming overwhelmed with bookkeeping and mailing, fundraising activities, or taxing editorial and production "bubbles." To find out more, about what we are doing, come see us at www.futurecycle.org.

www.ingramcontent.com/pod-product-compliance
Lightning Source LLC
Chambersburg PA
CBHW070452050426
42451CB00015B/3450